The Art of
Walking Bass

by Bob Magnusson

Contents

Introduction 2
The Basics 4

1: The Blues—Triads 9
2: The Blues—Diatonic Passing Tones 21
3: The Blues—Chromatic Tones 30
4: Minor Scales and Minor Blues 41
5: Rhythm Changes 45
6: Other Common Harmonic Progressions . . 53

Glossary 63
About the Author 64

All of the examples in this book are to be played in standard tuning, E–A–D–G, low to high.
The last track ❖ on the accompanying CD provides a series of notes to which you can tune up.

ISBN 978-0-7935-8042-2

CORPORATION
7777 W. BLUEMOUND RD. P.O. BOX 13819 MILWAUKEE, WI 53213

Visit Hal Leonard Online at
www.halleonard.com

INTRODUCTION

Walking bass lines are the building blocks, or foundation, upon which a song is laid. The term "walking" describes the feeling, or motion, of the bass line. Much like physical walking (one step after another), the continuous flow of quarter notes creates a feeling of forward momentum:

Walking bass lines are inherent to traditional jazz playing, but they are used in many other forms of music, too—blues, rock, R&B, gospel, country, classical, etc. Developing the ability to construct a good walking bass line can therefore only improve your choice of notes in creating any type of bass line. In all styles of music, the procedure used in building walking bass lines is essentially the same: Given a set of harmonies or chord changes, you, the bassist, must choose which notes to play and in what order to play them. The specific goal of this book is to help you understand the various techniques used to construct a good walking bass line. Armed with these techniques, you will then be able to build strong bass lines on your own as well as analyze bass lines and determine what makes some lines strong and others weak.

Here's how the book works...

Form

In my years of teaching, I've noticed that the *form* of a song is an area often overlooked by students; yet it is an essential part of almost all styles of music—just as any house has a blueprint, any song has a form. So, in this book, we'll learn how to play and write walking bass lines in the context of several common song forms. Specifically, we'll look at each of the following forms and progressions, covering them thoroughly:

- major blues
- minor blues
- II-V-I progressions
- rhythm changes
- other common harmonic progressions

The 3 Tonal Elements

As we learn these forms and progressions, we'll also look at the nuts and bolts of how to construct a walking bass line. We'll see that any walking bass line can be broken down into *three basic musical elements:*

- chord tones (arpeggios)
- diatonic tones (scale tones)
- chromatic tones (half steps)

We'll look at each of these elements separately, isolating exercises and examples to see how they work. Through this approach, we'll build our vocabulary gradually, understanding each individual element before moving on to the next—ultimately combining all three elements, and their various aspects, into one approach to create melodic walking bass lines.

How to Begin Practicing

The core of this book are the bass line exercises, each of which has its own audio track on the accompanying CD. For every exercise, you should analyze the bass line first, understand how it works, practice it on your own, and then play it along with the CD. In this way, you'll become thoroughly comfortable with it.

I'll then ask you to write your own bass line(s) for the same progression. In the beginning, when practicing to write your own bass lines, I highly recommend that you sit down with your bass and some sheets of manuscript paper. Then, **using your ear**, try to construct one, two, three, or four bars on your bass using the trial-and-error method. When you have a segment of any length that you like, write it down. Then play the part you've written, and continue on in this manner until your bass line is complete. In this way, your ear becomes an active part of the process, which is crucial to playing any improvised music. When your line is completed, *then* analyze harmonically what it is you've played. Through this method, you'll be able to establish a vocabulary in the walking bass language. You'll gradually build a group of phrases, licks, or ideas that sound good in various recurring harmonic situations. As your musical vocabulary grows, your trained ear will take over and guide you through some surprising and enjoyable excursions with walking bass lines.

Every improviser has thematic material or "licks" that they draw from to create a solo. Likewise, you can develop a set of ideas or phrases for your bass lines that fit various harmonic situations. Through the use of the recorded rhythm tracks on the accompanying CD, you'll have the opportunity to apply these ideas to a musical situation. In that way, you will be able to hear and feel how your bass line works.

For each audio track on the CD, the bass is on the left channel, and the rhythm section is on the right. To improvise your own bass part, turn your balance control to the right, and play along with just the rhythm section.

Good luck, and enjoy!

—Bob Magnusson

About the Compact Disc

When recording the compact disc for this book my aim was to create an environment as close to a live playing situation as possible. The tempos are in the medium slow range to give the student sufficient time to hear and perform the written lines. With the exception of examples 1 and 2, all the examples are repeated. Example 23 has a slow and a medium version while Section 6 includes medium tempos to coincide with the student's progress in constructing walking bass lines.

Each example is written solely in quarter notes in order to focus directly on the necessary techniques for constructing effective walking bass lines. Although I am reading the notated examples on the recording, the careful listener will notice how I utilize rhythmic anticipation and other nuances to add life to the music and facilitate interaction with the rhythm section.

Each track begins with Peter Erskine counting off the tempo. Mike Wofford generally comps sparsely on the first chorus and solos sparingly on the second. I know you will enjoy playing along with these two world-class musicians.

> For those with little to no experience in music theory, the following introductory section, entitled "The Basics," provides a crash course in intervals, scales, and chords, as well as a discussion of bass line contour and chord connection. Whatever your level—beginner or pro—I suggest you give this section a quick read-through before we get started... ☞

THE BASICS

Understanding Intervals

Interval: the distance between two notes.

Each interval name is made up of a combination of two elements:

1) *quantity*—The total number of letter names, or scale degrees, an interval contains. We determine this by counting the letter names, or lines and spaces, between the two notes, including the line or space the given notes are placed on. This gives us a general measurement. For example:

C to G

C, D, E, F, G. This is five letter names, so the interval is a 5th.

Now count the lines and spaces: 3 spaces + 2 lines = 5 total = the interval of a 5th

C to E

C, D, E. This is three letter names, so the interval is a 3rd.

Now count the lines and spaces: 2 spaces + 1 line = 3 total = the interval of a 3rd

| unison | 2nd | 3rd | 4th | 5th | 6th | 7th | octave |

2) *quality*—The total number of half steps contained in an interval. Quality gives us an exact measurement. Interval qualities are divided into two main groups:

<u>perfect</u>   <u>major and minor</u>

1 (unison), 4, 5, 8   2, 3, 6, 7

- When a major interval is decreased by one half step, it becomes a minor interval.

- When a minor interval is increased by one half step, it becomes a major interval.

- Perfect intervals never become major or minor intervals.

- *All* intervals (through the use of accidentals) can become augmented or diminished.

    a) When a minor or perfect interval is decreased by one half step, it becomes a diminished interval.

    b) When a major or perfect interval is increased by one half step, it becomes augmented.

To help you determine the quality of an interval, consider the following:

- If the top note of the interval belongs to the major scale of the lower note, the interval will be perfect or major.

- If the top note of the interval does not belong to the major scale of the lower note, compare the upper note to the scale tone with the same letter name.

For example:

C to G♯

The quantity of this interval is 5.

Is the top note of this interval (G♯) in the major scale of the lower note (C)? *No*

If not, is it higher or lower than the scale tone of the same name? *Higher*

By how much? *One half step*

What is the name of the interval? *Aug. 5*

Double sharps and double flats

It is occasionally necessary to use a double sharp or double flat in order to maintain the proper quantity when building an interval. These symbols are written as follows:

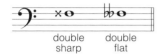

double   double
sharp   flat

Harmonizing the Major Scale

Harmonizing the major scale is a very simple process. First, you start by constructing a major scale. We'll use the key of C major because it has no sharps or flats:

C major scale

Now, using only the tones from the scale, build triads on each scale degree. This is done by stacking two thirds above each scale step. For instance, above the first note, C, we write the 3rd and 5th degrees of the scale:

   This forms a C major triad.

Moving up the scale to the second note, D, we write the 4th and 6th degrees of the scale:

   This forms a D minor triad.

And we continue this process for each scale step:

```
5    6    7    8    9
3    4    5    6    7
1    2    3    4    5    etc.
```

Here's how the C major scale looks, harmonized in triads:

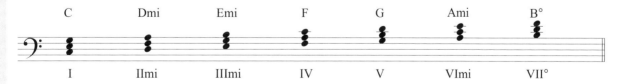

Notice that the scale position of each triad can be indicated by a large Roman numeral, and that the qualities of the triads are indicated with the suffixes "ma," "mi," or "°." The qualities of the triads in a harmonized major scale always follow this same formula, no matter what the key (C major, F major, B♭ major, etc.):

I	IImi	IIImi	IV	V	VImi	VII°

Harmonizing the Major Scale into Seventh Chords

Seventh chord: a four-note chord containing the three notes of the triad plus a fourth note—the interval of a 7th above the root.

This is the same process we used to harmonize the major scale into triads, only we will now add a 7th to each scale degree. We'll start by constructing a C major scale.

C major scale

Now using only the tones from the scale, we'll build diatonic seventh chords.

Each seventh chord has its own unique formula:

Chord type	Interval formula	Triad + 7th interval
ma7	root, ma3, P5, ma7	major triad + ma7
mi7	root, mi3, P5, mi7	minor triad + mi7
7	root, ma3, P5, mi7	major triad + mi7
mi7(♭5)	root, mi3, dim5, mi7	diminished triad + mi7

Notice that there are two important differences between triad harmony and seventh chord harmony:

- In triad harmony, the I, IV, and V chords are all the same quality, but in seventh chord harmony, the I and IV chords are major seventh chords (major triad + ma7 interval) whereas the V chord changes into a dominant seventh chord (major triad + mi7 interval).

- The VII chord changes from a diminished triad to a minor seventh flat-five chord (diminished triad + mi7 interval).

These seventh chord harmonies form the basis of our western tonal music.

Chord Symbols

Chord symbols are used as a musical shorthand. Due to regional variations, there are many different symbols that represent the same chord. However, some basic general rules are worth noting:

- A major triad is assumed when no symbol follows a chord letter. For example, the letter "C" by itself indicates a C major triad.

- The symbol "7" by itself, following any letter name, indicates a dominant seventh chord; for example, C7 indicates a major triad plus a minor 7th interval above the root—a.k.a., a C dominant seventh chord.

- The symbols "ma7," "ma9," or "ma13" show that a major 7th is included in the chord.

- The symbol "+" refers to the augmented 5th, not the augmented 9th or 11th. For example, C+9 means a C9 with an augmented 5th, not a C chord with an augmented 9th.

- All alterations should be written in parentheses; for example, C7(♭5) or C7(♭9). Chord symbols with several alterations are written with the highest harmonic function on top, within parentheses.

Name	Spelling	Symbols	Name	Spelling	Symbols
C major sixth		C6	C seven (flat nine)		C7(♭9), C7(-9)
C major seventh		Cma7, C△7, C7	C seven (sharp nine)		C7(♯9), C7(+9)
C major ninth		Cma9, C△9	C augmented seven		C+7, Caug7, C7(+5)
C minor sixth		Cmi6, C-6	C augmented nine		C+9, Caug9, C9(+5)
C minor seventh		Cmi7, C-7	C diminished seven		C°7, Cdim7
C minor ninth		Cmi9, C-9	C seven suspended fourth		C7sus, C$^7_4$, C7sus4
C minor seven (flat five)		Cmi7(♭5), C-7(♭5), CØ7	C nine suspended fourth		C7sus, C11, C9(♮11)
C minor nine (flat five)		Cmi9(♭5), C-9(♭5), CØ9	C minor eleven		Cmi11, C-11
C dominant seventh		C7	C seven sharp eleven		C7(♯11)
C dominant nine		C9, C$^9_7$	C minor seven over B♭		Cmi7/B♭, C-7/B♭

Smooth Transitional Connections

Transition refers to the movement that connects one chord to another (e.g., C to F) in a walking bass line. This most often occurs between the last beat of the chord you're playing and the first beat of the new chord. We'll be working on transitions throughout the book. *Usually,* the strongest motions to approach the first note of a new chord are for the bass line to go:

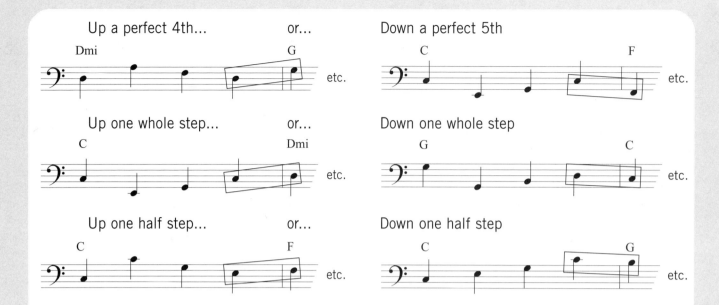

Contour and Line Direction

The **contour** or shape of a line becomes very important as your knowledge of constructing a bass line grows. We'll be referring to this aspect of building bass lines throughout this book as various musical situations arise.

There are a couple of aspects to consider when discussing contours. First, the shape or contour of a line can dictate our choice of connecting notes. For example:

Notice the contour of this line. Measure 1 rises up the Dmi7 arpeggio, and then, beginning on beat 4, descends diatonically (stepwise) through measure 2 to beat 1 of measure 3. This descending contour dictates that our first note of measure 3 be the 3rd of the new chord, E, instead of the root, C. This is a good example of the contour of your line dictating the choice of using a chord tone other than the root as your connecting tone. Notice the immediate outline of the C chord sound in measure 3.

Listen to the same line if we jump from the F (beat 4 of measure 2) to the root of the C chord (beat 1 of measure 3).

Hear how the whole flow and contour of the line is interrupted by jumping from the F to the C?

A second aspect to consider with contours is creating a **motif**—a basic recurring shape that can move through changing harmonic situations. The recurring motif need not be an identical duplication of the original idea, but a general or basic shape similarity. This creates a very musical bass line (like a recurring melody) that the ear grasps easily. Here's a brief example:

Just looking visually at the line, you can see the contour motif: from beat 1 to beat 2, a large jump upward; then beats 2, 3, and 4 fall off in a downward motion. Even though the harmony changes from one bar to the next, the basic shape or contour of the line remains the same. Listen with your ear to the continuity that the motif creates in the line.

Section ① The Blues—Triads

The blues is one of the most commonly used forms in all of popular music. For most of us, it's the form that we first jammed on in our various garage bands. Notice that it's twelve bars long and utilizes chords built on the 1st, 4th, 2nd, and 5th degrees of the major scale—in the key of C major, that's C, F, Dmi, and G.

Blues in C major

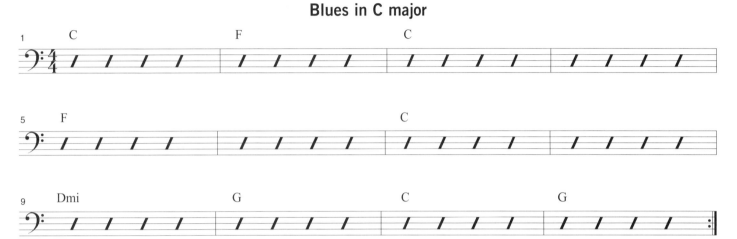

In this first exercise, we'll confine ourselves to using **only the triad** (root, 3rd, and 5th) of each chord with "no other tones allowed."

Ex. 1

While the bass line in exercise 1 is certainly functional (meaning that it outlines the harmony of the C blues), it is hardly musical (attractive to the ear). Notice that it is repetitive, in a redundant manner: the first three beats of all twelve bars are ascending up the root, 3rd, and 5th of each chord. Use your ear, and notice how monotonous this line is to listen to.

Exercise 2 is slightly more musical. Notice the shape or contour of the line. Even visually, it's more interesting.

② Ex. 2

We now have lines ascending and descending, which creates more contrast and color. But the line could be stronger if it had smoother connections between measures 2 and 3, 6 and 7, and 11 and 12. The key to doing this is to use inversions of triads.

Inversions

Inversions are created by simply rotating the order of the tones in a triad:

1, 3, 5 → 3, 5, 1 → 5, 1, 3 → 1, 3, 5

C Triad

F Triad

Dmi Triad

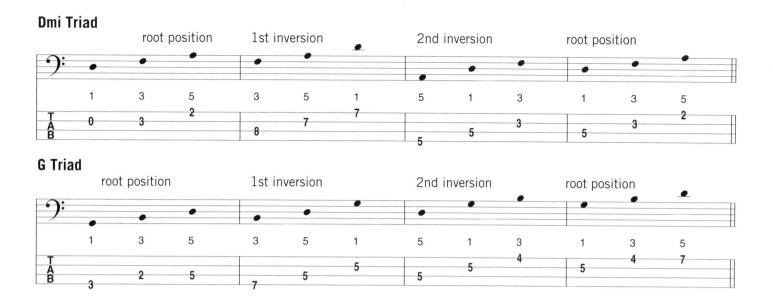

G Triad

The above inversions are in **closed position**. Another way to build or voice a triad is called open voicing, or **open position**. This simply means that, instead of having the tones of the triad as close together as possible, you space them out over a larger area, leaving space between tones where other chord tones could have resided.

C Triad

F Triad

Dmi Triad

G Triad

Now, armed with our new knowledge of inversions and open positions, let's create some really musical blues bass lines using "only the three tones of the triad."

◆3 **Ex. 3**

Sequences

Making a *sequence* from the three tones of a triad is a great way to create melodic interest—especially when a chord is *static* (standing still, not making a transition to another chord). Notice in the blues form how measures 3 and 4 remain static on the I chord (C), measures 5 and 6 remain static on the IV chord (F), and measures 7 and 8 remain static on the I chord again (C). These are good places to use sequences.

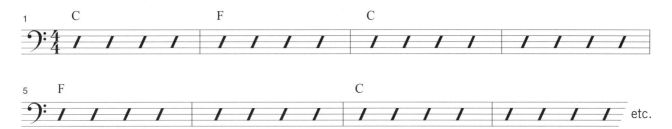

In fact, let's look at a few sequences that I used back in exercises 3 and 4. The first one occured in exercise 3, beat 3 of measure 3: a two-beat sequence that continued for six beats.

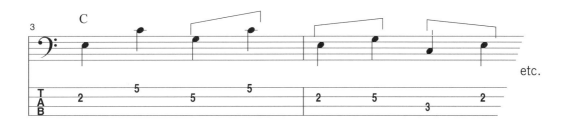

The next one occured in that same exercise, measures 7 and 8: a four-beat sequence.

The last one occured in exercise 4, measures 3 and 4. This is a four-beat sequence.

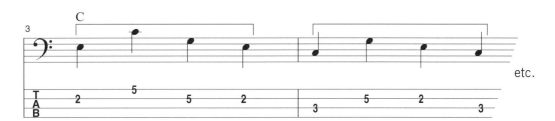

Basic Sequences

Following are sequences that re-cycle in various durations. Some are two-beat patterns, some are four-beat patterns, and some are eight-beat patterns. When you find one that you like, analyze the sequence of the chord tones (root, 3rd, 5th), and transpose it to other keys and other qualities (major, augmented, diminished).

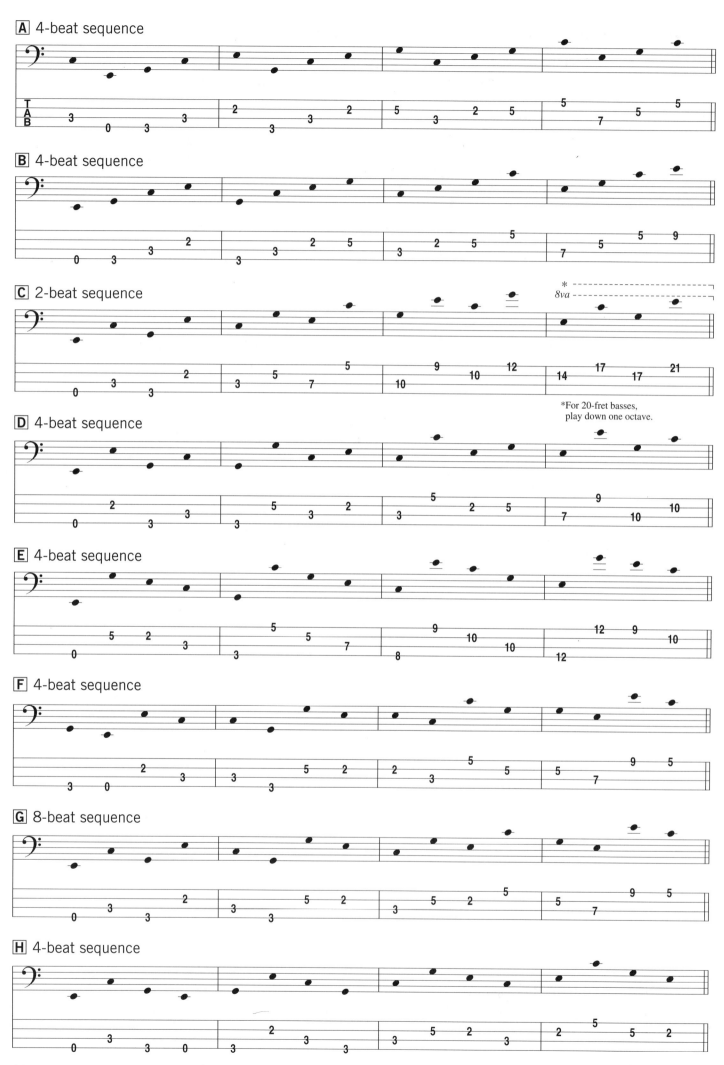

A 4-beat sequence

B 4-beat sequence

C 2-beat sequence

*For 20-fret basses,
play down one octave.

D 4-beat sequence

E 4-beat sequence

F 4-beat sequence

G 8-beat sequence

H 4-beat sequence

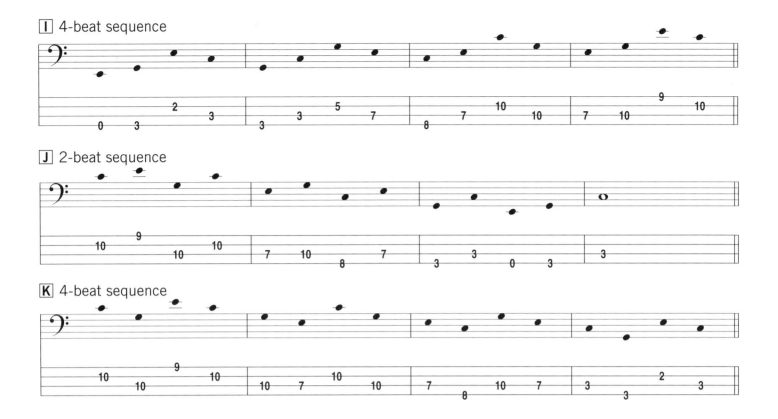

Basic Sequences—Backwards

Here are the same sequences, but in reverse.

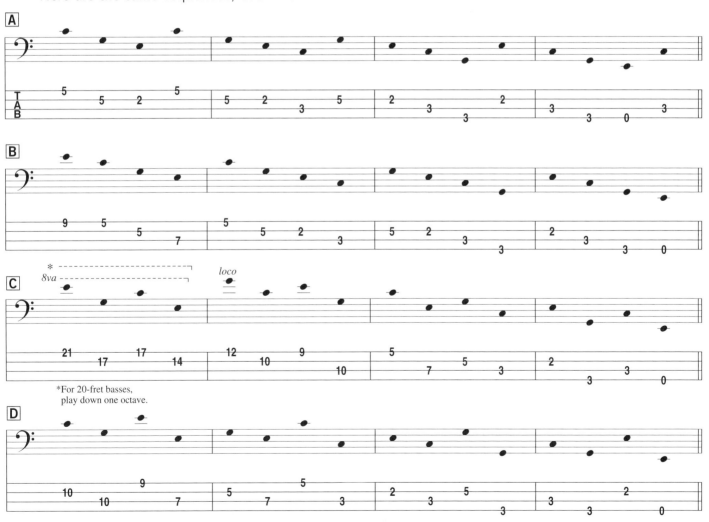

For Further Practice

When you're comfortable playing the blues bass lines in exercises 3 and 4—and can play them along with the rhythm section on the CD—try writing your own bass lines over the same basic blues progression using "only the triads" of the chords. Refer to page 3, "How to Begin Practicing," if you need help getting started.

The II-V-I Progression

The II-V-I progression is probably the most common harmonic motion in the standard repertoire. As the Roman numerals imply, it is a motion involving the II chord (built on the 2nd degree of the major scale), moving to the V chord (built on the 5th degree of the major scale), resolving to the I chord (built on the 1st degree of the major scale).

The next two exercises will apply this II-V-I progression moving through six keys each, **in triads only**.

5 ▶ Ex. 5

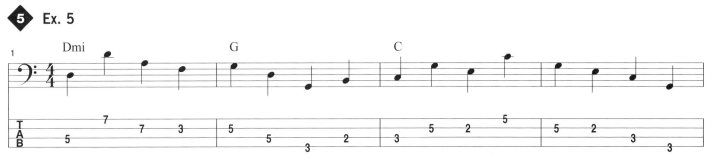

Ex. 6

For Further Practice

Once you can play along comfortably with the II-V-I bass lines I've given you, try writing your own bass lines over these progressions, using just the notes of each triad. Refer back to page 3 if you need help in getting started.

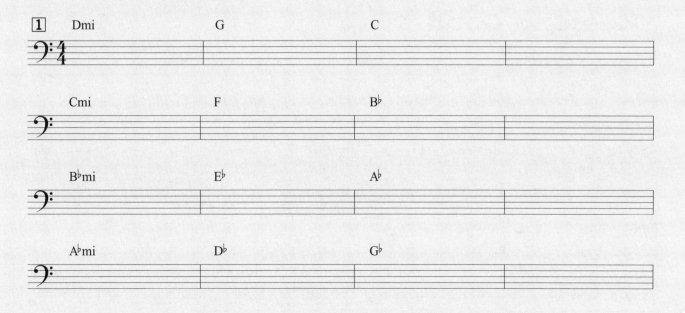

"Keeping Good Time"

The most important aspect of playing the bass is keeping good time. This is true in almost any style of popular music. No matter how great your musical approach, if your playing is not establishing a groove, it invalidates all the other qualities of your playing. As the late, great Duke Ellington said, "It don't mean a thing, if it ain't got that swing."

Playing along with the CD should help you in this regard. You can also begin to develop this aspect of your playing by practicing with a metronome. This will help you to develop a sense of evenness in your time. Don't be discouraged if it's not coming right away. Remember: playing good solid time involves knowledge of the fingerboard, technical command of your instrument, and hearing the phrase you want to play.

Besides using the metronome and playing along with the CD, listen to recordings of some of the great bassists. Study and try to absorb their sense of swing. Try to play with as many good drummers as possible, and work to lock-up your groove with theirs. All of these aspects will help you develop your inner clock and get you on the road to playing great time.

Section 2 — The Blues—Diatonic Passing Tones

Diatonic passing tones are notes derived from the scale corresponding to the chord that you are playing—apart from the chord tones themselves, that is.

Here are the scales that correspond to the four chords we've been using to outline a C blues progression. The diatonic passing tones are circled:

*These are not "major" and "minor" scales, but are modal scales built from the C major scale.

Notice that all scale tones for this blues progression are derived from the C major scale, so if you know one scale, you know them all. However, for the C and F scales, you may also use a minor seventh—B♭ in the C scale, E♭ in the F scale. This is a characteristic sound of the blues progression. (Actually, it's the ♭7th of the dominant seventh chord, which we'll see more of later.) Use your ear to pick the sound or sounds that you like best.

In this chapter, we'll also be adding two more chords to our basic blues progression: Emi and A. These will add some color and harmonic motion to our basic progression:

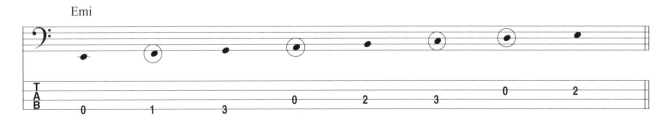

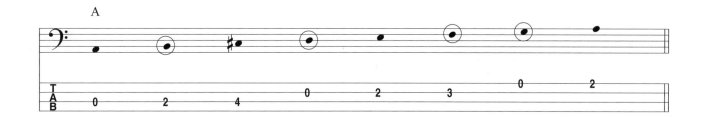

Notice below that measures 7-8 now move I-IV-IIImi-VI, and measures 11-12 move I-VI-IImi-V. These are common harmonic motions used in the blues to create more color.

7 **Ex. 7**

- Notice the stepwise motion of measure 2, the four notes from beat 2 of measure 6 to beat 1 of measure 7, and the five notes from beat 3 of measure 7 to beat 3 of measure 8.

- Notice the repeated four-note sequence used in measures 9 and 10. (It also begins the line in measure 1.)

Exercise 8 uses sequences extensively.

8 **Ex. 8**

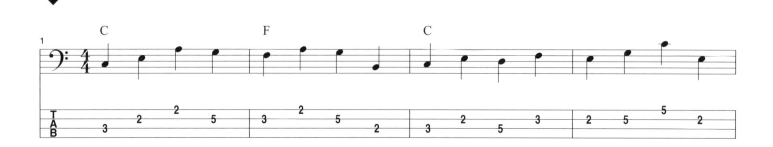

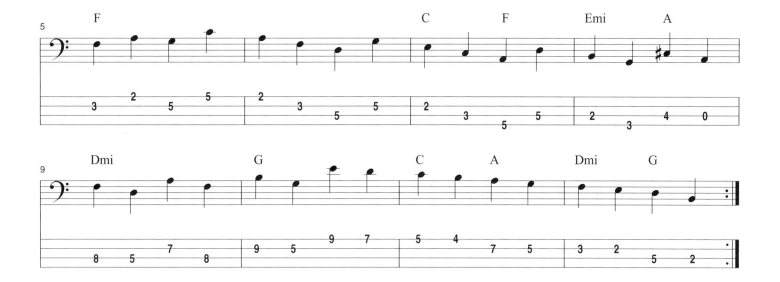

- Notice the two-beat sequence of ascending major and minor thirds in measure 3 and beats 1 and 2 of measure 4; then, starting on the third beat of measure 5, a four-beat sequence occurring three times, ending on the second beat of measure 8; overlapping a two-beat sequence of major and minor thirds occurring five times, ending on the second beat of measure 10.

- Compare the two sequences of thirds. Notice the first sequence in measures 3 and 4, where the third intervals ascend as does the sequence. But in the second sequence (measures 8, 9, and 10), the third interval descends while the two-beat sequence ascends.

Exercise 9 combines large intervals with stepwise motion to create an interesting bass line. The stepwise motion occurs in measure 4 to measure 5, measure 5 to measure 6, and measure 9 to measure 10.

9 **Ex. 9**

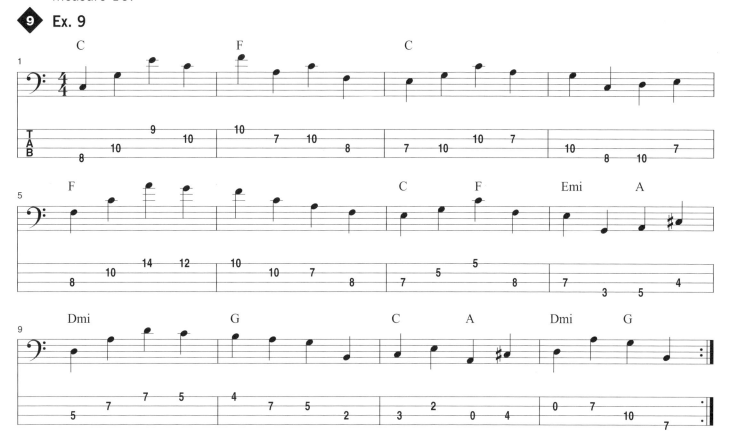

- Notice the contour of measure 8. Even though beats 2, 3, and 4 are not all stepwise, it creates the same feeling of stepwise movement that measure 4 has.

- Notice how many times I've used intervals of fifths and sixths, sometimes back to back, to create the open feeling this line contains.

Bypassing Changes

Because we've added more harmonic motion to our blues progression than we had in earlier examples, I'd like to share a concept with you that has been very important to me over the years. I like to use the illustration of two trains.

The first train is the "local"; it stops in every little town. The second train is an "express"; it bypasses the small towns and only stops in the larger, more important cities. Our concept of constructing a bass line can be like these two trains, with the chords of the progression representing the cities and towns. When we construct a bass line and take the "local," our bass line goes to and outlines every single chord. When we take the "express," our bass line can bypass chords that are there to add color and create more motion, and go directly to the more important chords.

To see how to apply this concept, let's look back at exercises 8 and 9. Here in exercise 8, measures 7 and 8, I've taken the "express." I'm not clearly outlining every chord change.

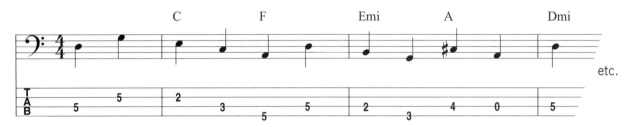

This occurred because of a sequence I was using that began on beat 3 of measure 5. In this case, the strength of the line contour allowed me to bypass the F and Em chords.

Here in measures 7 and 8 of exercise 9, I've taken the "local." Notice that each chord change is clearly outlined.

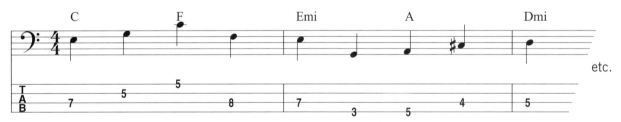

Now notice measures 11 and 12 of these two exercises. Here in exercise 8, measures 11 and 12, I've taken the "express."

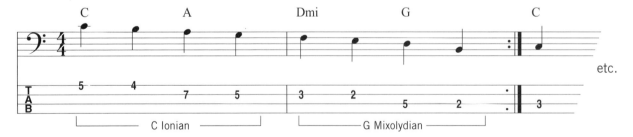

Rather than outline the A and Dmi chords, I heard this line moving from the C chord, diatonically descending through the G chord, and arriving at the target note C in measure 13. Notice the strong, downward contour of the line.

Here in measures 11 and 12 of exercise 9, I've taken the "local." Notice how the bass line clearly outlines each chord change.

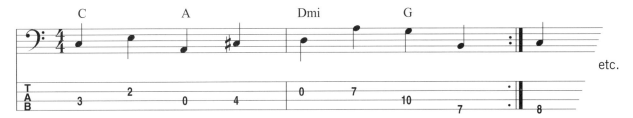

For Further Practice

Practice the blues bass lines in exercises 7, 8, and 9 until you can play them comfortably along with the CD. Then try writing your own lines. Remember: we've added chord changes in measures 7–8 and 11–12, create a slightly more sophisticated blues progression. Feel free to take the "local" or the "express only." Use notes of the triad plus diatonic passing tones, and watch the contours of your line.

The Diatonic Modes

The diatonic modes are essential to learn as you begin building your scale vocabulary. These modes are constructed from each of the seven degrees of the major scale, using only notes of the key you've chosen. We'll construct them in the key of C major, as it has no sharps or flats and will be easy to visualize.

Practice these modes in all twelve keys to get familiar with the way that they sound and feel.
NOTE: Each mode corresponds to the chord built on the same scale degree.

The II-V-I Progression

Let's work on our II-V-I changes, adding diatonic passing tones to our vocabulary. Each exercise moves through six keys.

Ex. 10

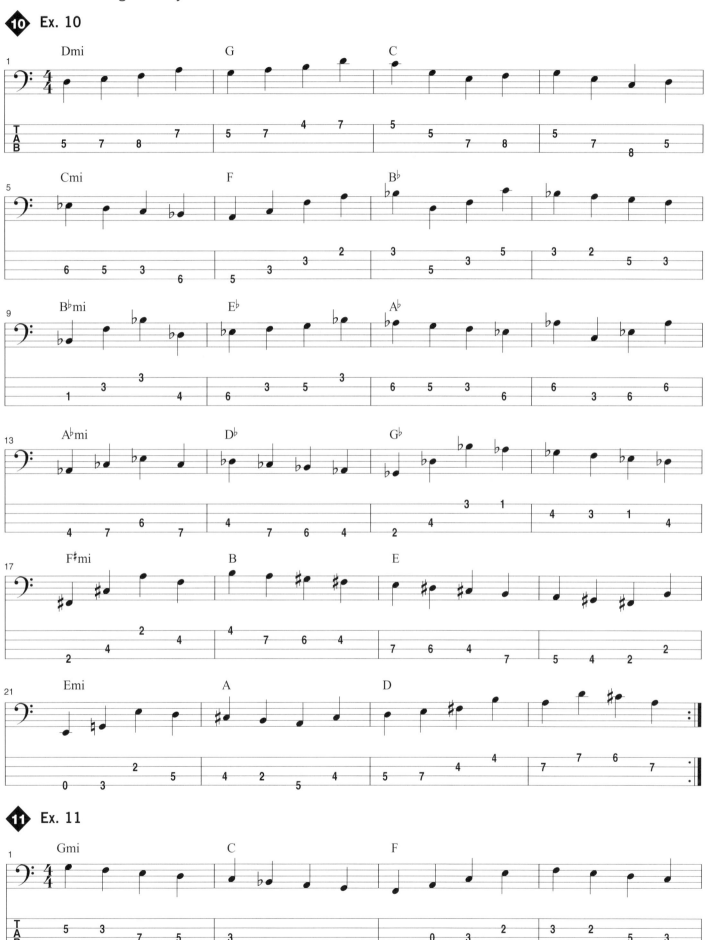

Ex. 11

For Further Practice

When you can play exercises 10 and 11 comfortably along with the rhythm section on the CD, it's time to try writing your own bass lines over these II-V-I progressions. Remember: only use the notes of each triad *plus* diatonic passing tones. Think about the contours of your line.

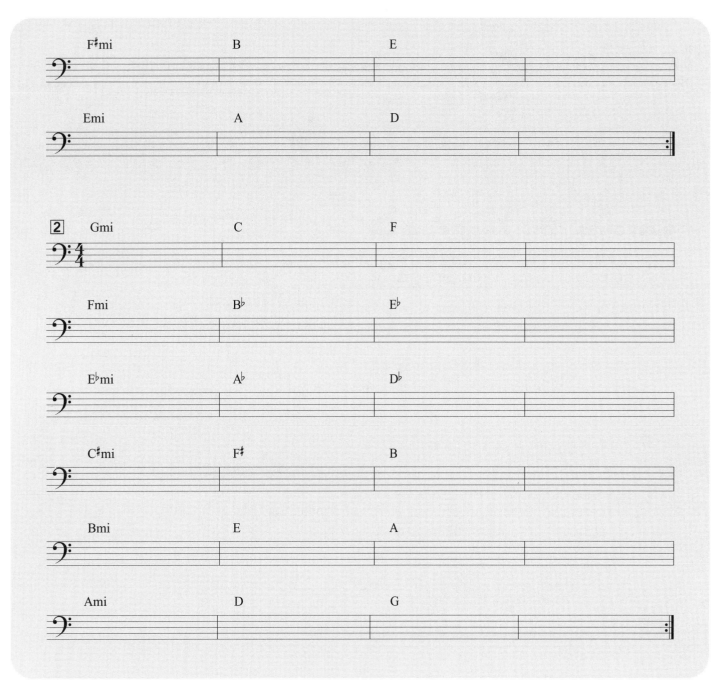

Section 3 · The Blues—Chromatic Tones

Chromatic tones can be used in several ways in conjunction with triads to outline the blues. In this section, we'll break down each of these techniques and apply them to an F blues progression.

Chromatic Approach

In the first method, chromatic approach, a chromatic tone approaches the target note (root, 3rd, or 5th of the triad) from either a half step above or below.

For example, here, the bass line ascends up the triad (root, 3rd, 5th) and then on beat 4 uses a chromatic tone (B♮) to approach the target note (B♭) from a half step above:

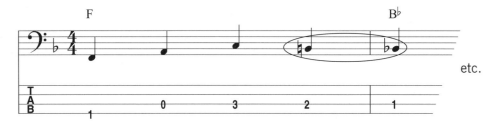

In this next example, the first three beats are chord tones (root, 5th, root), then beat 4 is a chromatic approach from below to the target note (B♭):

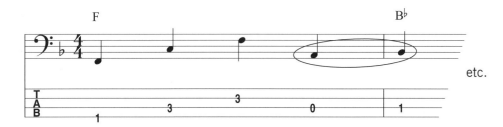

Notice that this A♮ is both a chromatic approach tone to B♭ and the 3rd of the F chord. A chromatic approach tone does not always have to be outside the tonality—it may be a chord tone, too, and still achieve the same effect.

Chromatic approach tones may go to other chord tones besides the root, as well. For example, here, the chromatic approach tone (E♭) moves to the the 3rd of the next chord (D, the 3rd of B♭) from above.

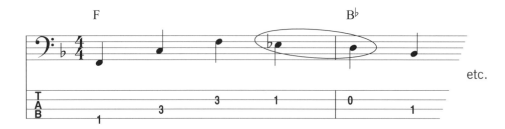

And here, the chromatic approach tone (C#) moves to the 3rd (D) of the next chord from below.

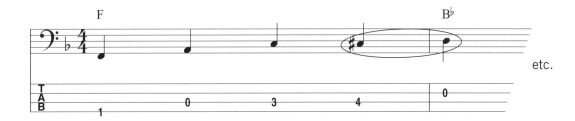

The chromatic approach tones we've seen so far have all occurred at a transition point (one chord moving to another), but chromatic approach tones may also be used in a static situation, within a single chord. The same principle applies; the chromatic approach tone always moves to a chord tone.

This example represents measures 3, 4, and 5 of an F blues. Notice in measure 3 that we have two static chromatic approaches: B♮ (chromatic approach from below) to the target note C (the 5th) and G♭ (chromatic approach from above) to the target note F (the root).

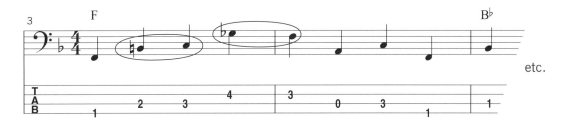

In exercises 12 and 13, I've circled all the transitional and static chromatic approaches so you can clearly get a grasp on how this technique is used. Study them closely with your eye and your ear before writing your own bass line.

Ex. 12

Notice the four beat sequence in bar 9 and 10.

- Notice in exercise 13, measures 1, 2, and 3, how I've combined a four-beat contour motif with the chromatic approach.

13 **Ex. 13**

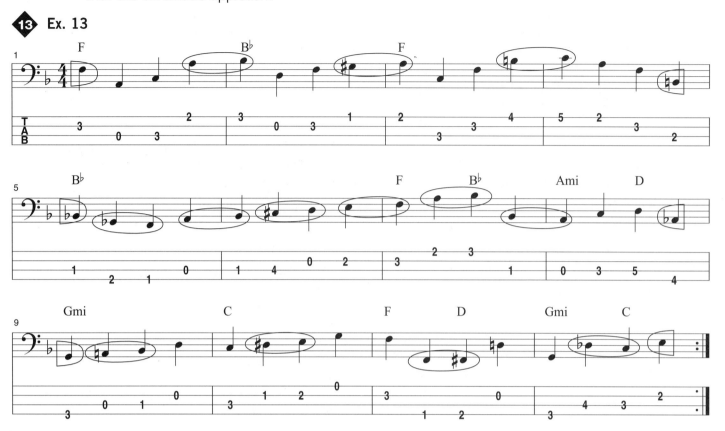

For Further Practice

When you can play along comfortably with exercises 12 and 13, try writing your own bass lines in this style. Use only notes of the triad plus chromatic approach tones—try using them in both transitional and static situations.

Chromatic Surround

Another aspect of chromatic approach is to surround the target note with chromatic tones above and below the target note—or the reverse, below and above. This technique can be used in transition to another chord or in a static situation when the chord stands still.

This first example is in transition, with the target note being the Bb in measure 2. Notice the two chromatic tones on beats 3 and 4 of measure 1. The B♮ is above, the A is below, completely surrounding the target note Bb.

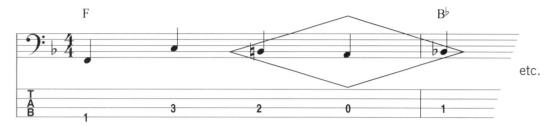

This one is also in transition, but now the chromatic surround is in reverse. The chromatic tone (A) below the target is played first, and the chromatic tone above (B♮) is played next.

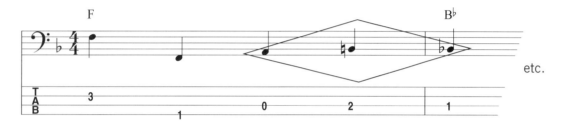

Here are measures 3-5 of an F blues. Notice that the static chromatic surround moves from above (Bb) to below (G♯) on beats 3 and 4 of measure 3. Because the F chord is static throughout measures 3 and 4, the A♮ (3rd of the F chord) on beat 1 of measure 4 is the target note.

This example is also measures 3-5 of an F blues. Notice that the static chromatic surround moves from below (E♮) to above (Gb) on beats 3 and 4 of measure 3. Because the F chord is static through measures 3 and 4, the F♮ (root of F chord) is the target note.

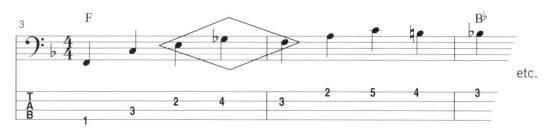

In exercises 14 and 15, the "chromatic approaches" are circled, and the "chromatic surrounds" are in diamonds.

14 **Ex. 14**

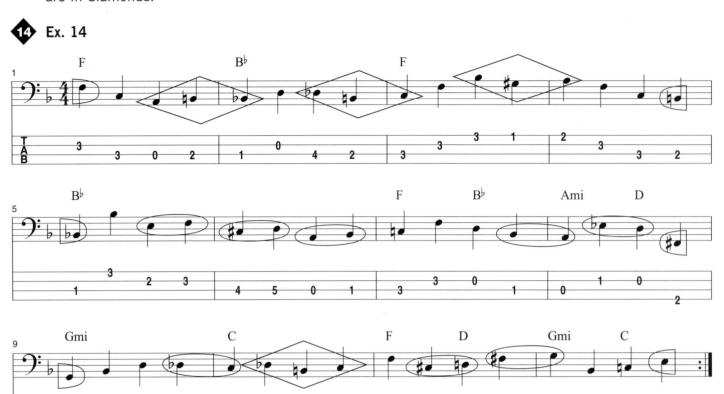

15 **Ex. 15**

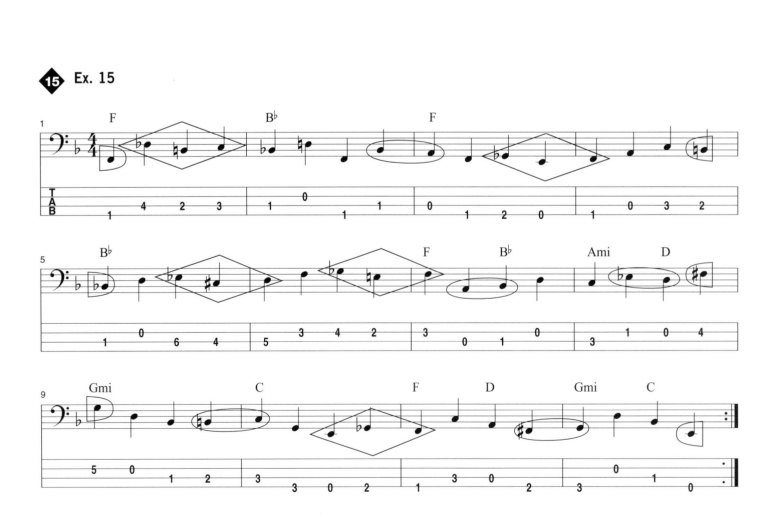

For Further Practice

When you can play along comfortably with exercises 14 and 15, try writing your own bass lines using only notes of each triad plus chromatic approach tones and chromatic surrounds.

Chord-Tone-to-Chord-Tone

The final phase of chromatic approach is to move chromatically from one chord tone to another. This can occur within the same chord (static) or while one chord moves to another (transitions).

Our first example is measures 3-4 of an F blues, where the F chord remains static. Notice the chromatic line begins on A, the 3rd of the F chord (beat 2 of measure 3) and moves chromatically up to C, the 5th of the F chord (beat 1 of measure 4).

This next one is also measures 3-4 of an F blues. Notice the chromatic line begins on A, the 3rd (beat 1 of measure 3) and moves chromatically down to F, the root (beat 1 of measure 4).

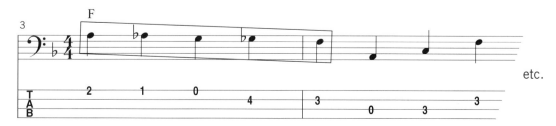

Here are measures 1-3 of an F blues. Notice in measure 1 that the line starts with a whole step and then begins the chromatic motion. The whole step is essential to arrive on time at the target note (B♭) on beat 1 of measure 2. This is a common chromatic motif when chords move up in perfect fourths. Measure 2 moves from the 3rd of the B♭ chord (D), chromatically up to the root of the F chord (F) on beat 1 of measure 3.

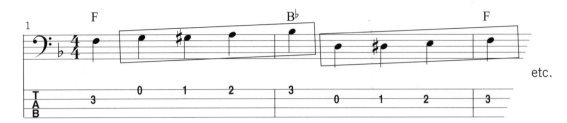

Exercises 16 and 17 are both F blues, using triads and all facets of chromatic approach.

- Chromatic approaches are circled.
- Chromatic surrounds are in diamonds.
- Chromatic chord-tone-to-chord-tone lines are in boxes.

16 Ex. 16

17 Ex. 17

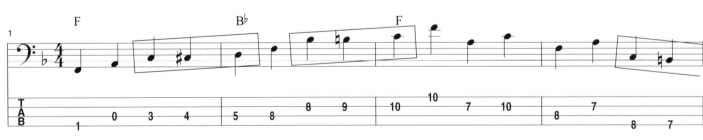

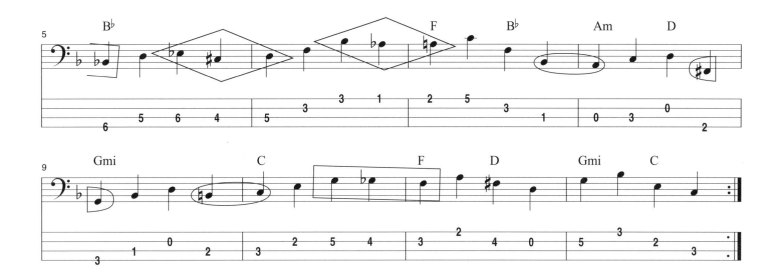

For Further Practice

When you can play along comfortably with exercises 16 and 17, write your own bass lines. Use only notes of each triad, plus chromatic approaches, chromatic surrounds, and chromatic chord-tone-to-chord-tone lines.

The II-V-I Progression

Analyze and then play these II-V-I progressions.

- Chromatic approaches are circled.
- Chromatic surrounds are in diamonds.
- Chromatic chord-tone-to-chord-tone lines are in boxes.

Ex. 18

Ex. 19

For Further Practice

When you can play along comfortably with the II-V-I progressions in exercises 18 and 19, write your own II-V-I bass lines using only notes of each triad plus all the chromatic techniques we've learned—chromatic approach, chromatic surround, and chromatic chord-tone-to-chord-tone.

Section ④ Minor Scales and Minor Blues

Minor Scales

C natural minor or pure minor (a.k.a., the C Aeolian mode)

C harmonic minor

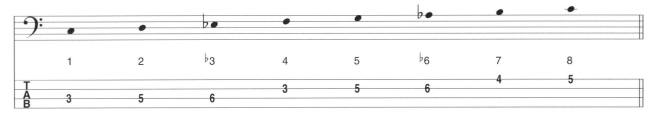

Notice the augmented 2nd interval between scale steps 6 and 7; this gives the harmonic minor scale its characteristic sound.

C melodic minor

Notice that this is just like the C major scale, but with a minor 3rd.

Pentatonic Scales

Pentatonic scales are scales containing only five tones. (The name is derived from the Greek word "penta," meaning "five.") There are many pentatonic scales but these two are the most commonly used.

C major pentatonic   C minor pentatonic

Minor Blues

Minor blues are very much like major blues, except that they're built on a minor tonality; both types consist of a twelve-bar form. A variation often occurs, however, in measure 9 of the minor blues, where composers frequently prefer the sound of the ♭VI7 chord to that of the IImi7(♭5) chord.

Blues in C minor

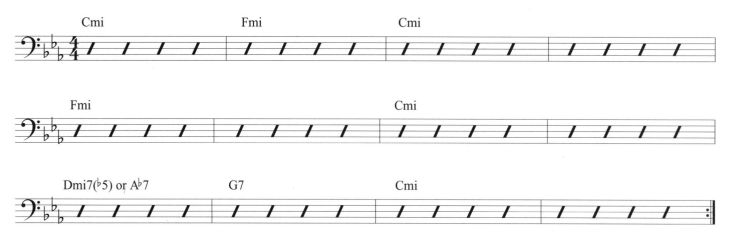

We will use both chords in our examples so your ear can hear the difference. Also, minor blues, like major blues, can have varying harmonic motions to connect the main points of the form. In exercises 20–22, I've used a few different variations.

From here on out, we'll use all three facets of walking bass: arpeggios, diatonic passing tones, and chromatic tones. Also, all harmonies will be based on seventh chords.

20 Ex. 20

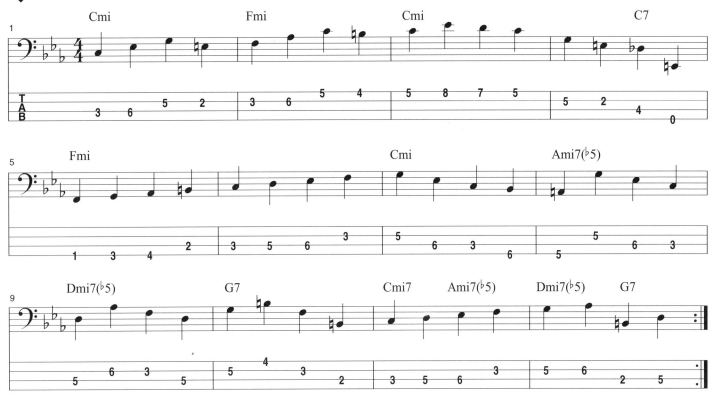

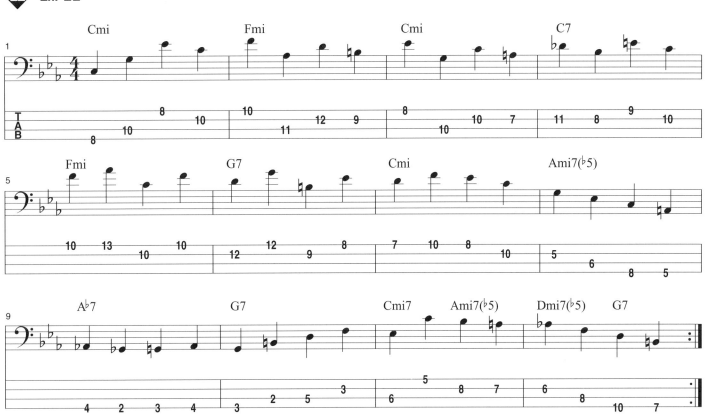

For Further Practice

When you're comfortable playing along with exercises 20–22, try writing your own bass lines over a C minor blues progression. Remember: you can use seventh chord arpeggios, diatonic passing tones (from any of the C minor scales), and chromatic tones to help shape your lines.

Section 5 — Rhythm Changes

AABA Form

After the blues, "rhythm changes" are probably the most widely used set of chord changes in improvised music. Rhythm changes comprise a 32-bar form, divided into four 8-bar sections. The first eight bars (called the A section) state the melodic theme. The second eight bars (also an A section) repeat the theme. The third eight bars (called the B section) establish a contrasting melody and set of chord changes. The fourth and final eight bars (also an A section) are a return to the opening theme.

Incidentally, the chords to this popular progression come from the classic Gershwin tune "I Got Rhythm"—hence the term, rhythm changes.

Rhythm changes in B♭

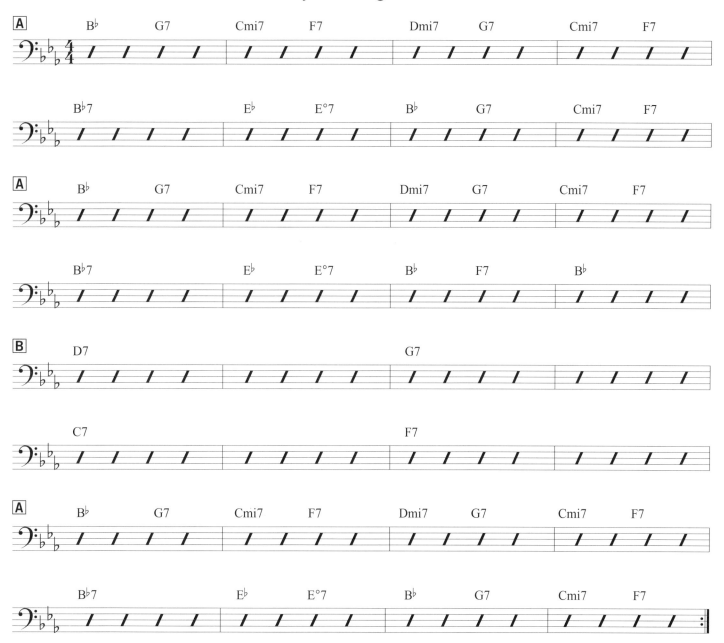

This 32-bar song form is referred to as an AABA form. It was one of the most widely used song forms by our great American composers—George Gershwin, Jerome Kern, Cole Porter, Irving

Berlin, Harold Arlen, etc. Whenever you're learning a new song, always examine the form, so you have a picture of the shape of the song in your mind's eye. This will help you remember the song and also be able to transpose it to another key.

Notice how the harmonies in the A sections move almost exclusively in two-beat patterns, while the B section harmonies move in two-bar patterns. Play through, listen, and analyze how the bass line moves through these quick-moving, two-beat chord changes in exercise 23.

23 **Ex. 23**

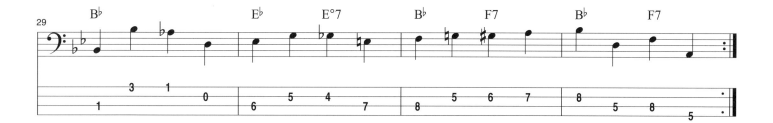

- Observe measures 6-7, 14-15, and 30-31. Use your ear and notice that the line contour leads the bass line to the note F (the 5th) on the B♭ chord change. To have placed the note B♭ (the root) on the downbeat would have interrupted the flow and continuity of the line.

24 Ex. 24

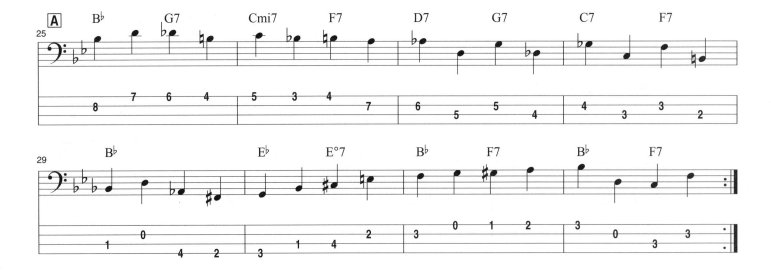

Exercise 24 is much more adventurous than exercise 23. A line like this would be played behind a soloist that is "stretching out" on the chord changes. Notice some techniques I've used:

- measures 1 and 2—major 3rds ascending chromatically

- measures 7-12—a four-beat descending melodic sequence

- measure 25 (beats 3-4) and measure 26—chromatic surround

- measures 27-28—descending chromatic sequence

Also notice some harmonic variations compared to exercise 23:

- measures 17-24—instead of two measures of each dominant chord, we precede each dominant chord with its IImi7 chord.

- measures 27-28—all four chords are dominant seventh chords.

For Further Practice

When you can play along comfortably with exercises 23 and 24, try writing your own bass lines over these rhythm changes in B♭. Use everything—arpeggios, diatonic passing tones, and chromatic tones.

No. 1

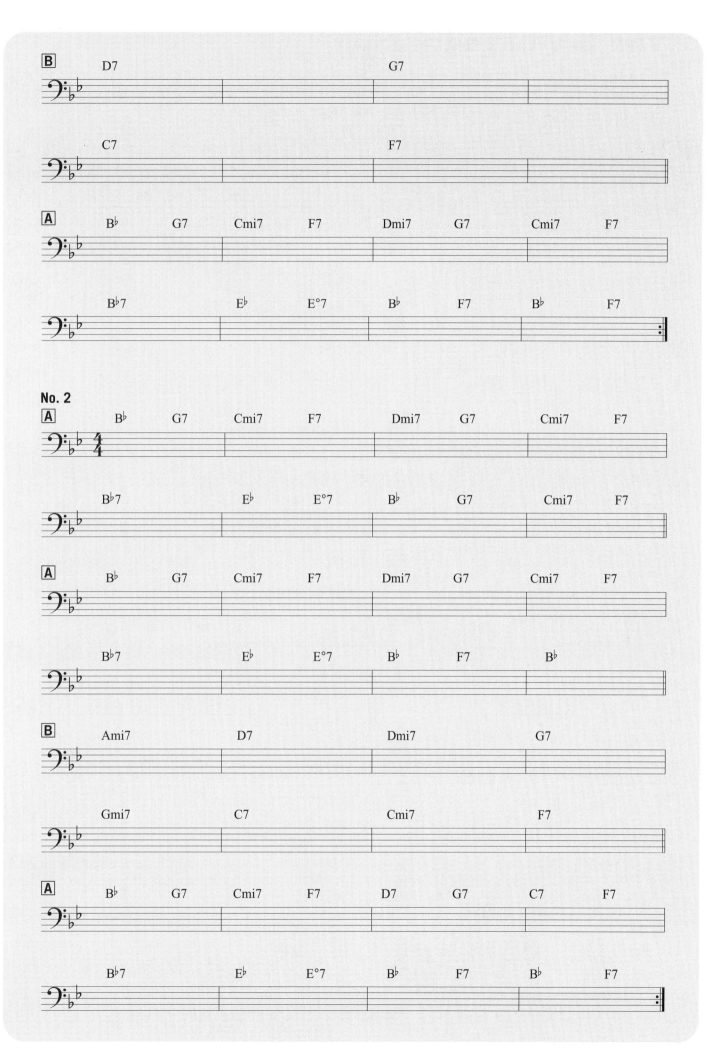

The II-V-I Progression

These II-V-I bass lines use everything we've learned—arpeggios, diatonic passing tones, and chromatic tones. Notice that we're outlining the II-V-I progression using seventh chords now instead of just triads. Analyze these lines, and then start playing them.

 Ex. 25

26 Ex. 26

51

For Further Practice

When you can play along comfortably with the II-V-I bass lines in exercises 25 and 26, try writing your own. Think in terms of seventh chords, and add diatonic passing tones and chromatic tones to shape your lines.

Section 6 — Other Common Harmonic Progressions

Using Chord Tones Outside the Key Center

Over the years, this concept has worked very well; I find that students grasp the idea and can use it almost immediately. Here it is: first, take a tune or progression you're working on, and write out (or mentally visualize) all the seventh chords in the piece. For example:

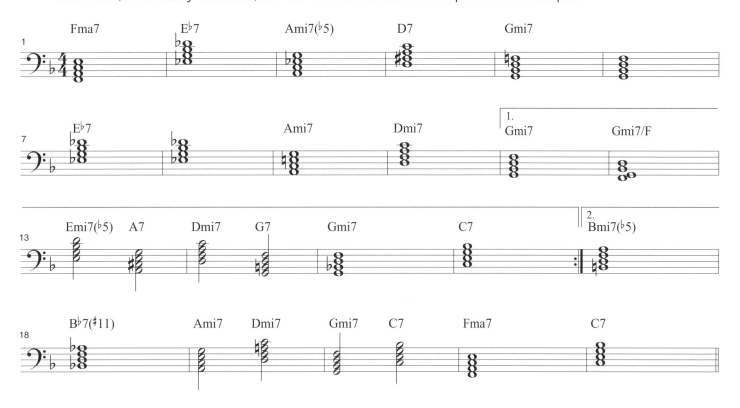

Now, write out the major (or minor) scale of the key center. Our progression is in the key of F major:

F major scale

Now simply go through your harmonized progression and pick out the chord tones that are not in your key center scale. For example:

- Measure 2 has two notes that are not in the F major scale, E♭ and D♭.
- Measure 3 has E♭.
- Measure 4 has F♯.
- Measures 7-8 have E♭ and D♭.
- The second half of measure 13 has C♯.
- The second half of measure 14 has B♮.
- Measure 17 has B♮.
- Measure 18 has A♭.

Now examine the bass line I've written for this progression, and notice how I've incorporated these chord tones from outside the key center into my bass line. This is a 32-bar progression with an ABAC form. Each section is eight bars long. The two A sections are identical, while the B and C sections are contrasting.

27 Ex. 27

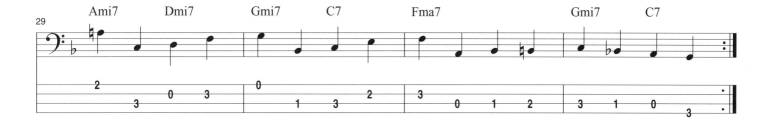

- Notice in measures 19-21 the use of large intervals to create a feeling of root motion on beats 1 and 4, and chord colors on beats 2 and 3.

- Observe the contour sequence in measures 27-31.

For Further Practice

When you're comfortable playing along with exercise 27, try writing your own bass line, using this same concept. Think of the chord tones that are outside the key center as little jewels adding new colors to your harmonic palette.

More Common Harmonic Progressions

Here's a 32-bar progression with an AABC form. Each section is eight bars long. Notice the use of the ♭9 on the dominant chords in measures 2, 14, 18, and 26. Notice the places where I've used sequences: measures 3-4, 5-6, 9-10, and 15-16.

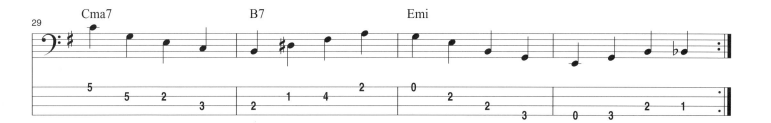

For Further Practice

When you can play along comfortably with exercise 28, try writing your own bass line on this progression. Use chord tones outside the key center to color your lines.

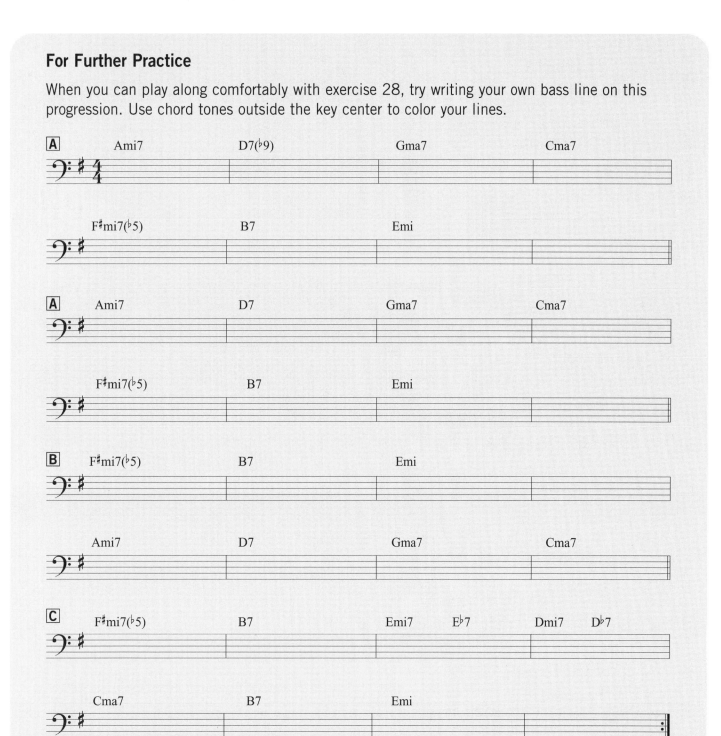

Here's a 32-bar progression with an AABA form. Each section is eight bars long. Notice in the A sections how the Cma7 and D7(♯11) remain static for two bars, and in the B section, the Fma7 remains static for four bars. Analyze how this bass line deals with those areas.

* Notice I take the "express" through measures 31 and 32.

For Further Practice

When you're comfortable playing along with exercise 29, try writing your own bass line on this progression.

Here's a 32-bar progression with an ABAC form. Each section is eight bars long.

30 **Ex. 30**

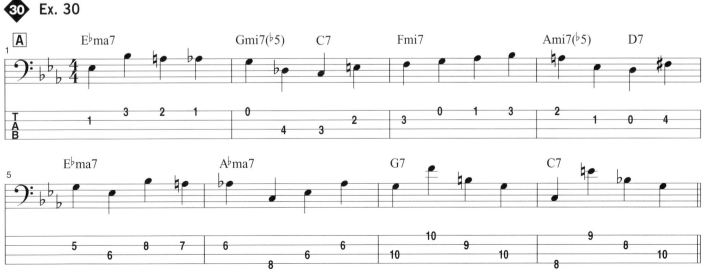

- Notice the duplication of the chromatic motif in measures 17 and 19.

For Further Practice

When you're comfortable playing along with exercise 30, try writing your own bass line over this progression.

Here's a 32-bar progression with an AABA form. Each section is eight bars long. Notice the rapid key changes in the B section—B♭ major, G♭ major, D major, G♭ major, and back to F major. In an area like this, be sure to clearly outline these rapid key changes so the soloist can hear the changing tonalities. Except for two passing tones (measures 19 and 21), this bass line is all chord tones throughout the B section.

31 Ex. 31

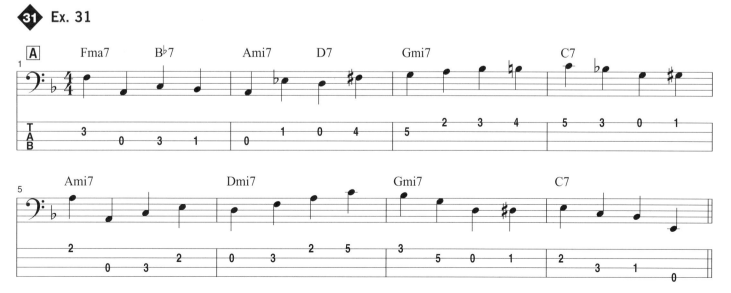

For Further Practice

When you're comfortable playing along with exercise 31, try writing your own bass line over this progression.

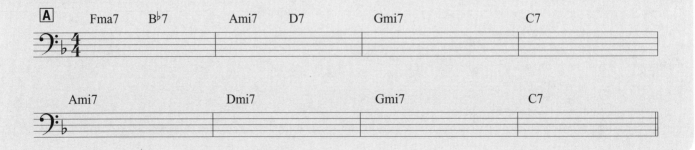

Glossary

arpeggio: A chord in which the notes are played in succession, rather than simultaneously.

motif: A theme or lick of any length.

static: Remaining on the same chord.

transition: Moving from one chord to another.

8va: Played one octave higher than written.

loco: Played where written.

diatonic: Notes from within a scale.

interval: The distance between two pitches.

target note: The pitch towards which a melodic line is heading.

chromatic: Moving by half steps.

sharp (♯): Raises a note by one half step.

flat (♭): Lowers a note by one half step.

natural (♮): Cancels a previous sharp or flat.

accidental: A sharp, flat, or natural, not diatonic to the key.

key: A tonal, or pitch, center.

augment: To enlarge.

diminish: To make smaller.

double flat (𝄫): Lowers a note by one whole step.

double sharp (𝄪): Raises a note by one whole step.

transpose: Change to a different key.

repeat signs: (𝄆▬𝄇) = Repeat all bars within the signs. (𝄎) = Repeat chord from previous bar.

About the Author

Born in New York City on February 24, 1947, Bob Magnusson was raised in a musical family. He first began studying French horn at age six and continued for twelve years until as a teenager, he discovered guitar and began playing electric bass in rock bands. By 1965, he was in a San Diego based R&B band and there had his first exposure to jazz: Miles Davis's *Kind of Blue*. Shortly thereafter, he purchased an acoustic bass and began to learn to play.

In 1968 he joined the Buddy Rich Band for a year. In 1971-72 and 1975-76 he worked with the Sarah Vaughan Trio, performing with the renowned drummer Jimmy Cobb. Moving to Los Angeles in 1975, Bob was actively performing and recording with the Art Pepper Quartet, Benny Golson Quartet, and the Joe Farrell Quartet.

After an extensive career performing in show bands, jazz, clubs, and symphonies on both the West and East coasts and abroad, Bob also gained notoriety as a teacher and clinician (he was an active faculty member of Musicians Institute in Hollywood from 1977-1996). He moved back to San Diego in 1983, where he currently resides with his wife and family. Since that time, he has recorded two dozen KPBS jazz specials for television, and otherwise keeps busy playing and recording. His personal discography lists in excess of 100 albums and CDs to his credit, including recordings by such fine pop artists as Linda Ronstadt, Neil Diamond, Bonnie Raitt, 10,000 Maniacs, and Madonna. He has also performed with numerous jazz greats, including Hank Jones, Cedar Walton, Jimmy Heath, Art Farmer, Kenny Barron, Freddie Hubbard, Slide Hampton, Billy Higgins, Carl Fontana, Tommy Flanagan, Kenny Burrell, Roger Kellaway, Ernie Watts, Eddie "Cleanhead" Vinson, Lou Donaldson, Joe Henderson, Clifford Jordan, George Cables, Victor Lewis, Bud Shank, and many others.

In 1983, Bob was honored by the San Diego Hall of Fame as the "Jazz Player of the Year."

About the Musicians

Mike Wofford entered the Los Angeles music scene in the late fifties and early sixties with the legendary Lighthouse All-Stars and the bands of Shelly Manne, Teddy Edwards, Chet Baker, Zoot Sims, Bud Shank, Sonny Criss, and Shorty Rogers, among others. Over the following years he has appeared and recorded with such artists as Kenny Burrell, Stan Getz, Lee Konitz, Joe Henderson, Harry "Sweets" Edison, Slide Hampton, Benny Golson, Art Farmer, Charlie Haden and Joe Pass. In 1979 and 1983 he was Sarah Vaughan's pianist and conductor. From 1989 to 1992 he was the Musical Director and pianist for Ella Fitzgerald. In addition, Mike has recorded ten solo albums of his own. *Downbeat Magazine* called him "one of the outstanding pianists of our time" and noted music critic Leonard Feather wrote "Wofford now occupies a plateau alongside precious few others."

Peter Erskine has been at the forefront of world-class ensembles for over 26 years. In 1972 to 1975 he played with the Stan Kenton Orchestra, in 1976 and 1977 he was the drummer with the Maynard Ferguson Big Band, and in 1978 he joined Weather Report. The excellence of the partnership between Peter and bassist Jaco Pastorius was an integral part of that group's success. After four years with Weather Report, Peter joined Michael Brecker in the group Steps Ahead. His other touring and recording credits (300 albums) include Steely Dan, Chick Corea, Joe Henderson, Freddie Hubbard, Gary Burton, Pat Metheny, and Joni Mitchell. Peter has recorded 12 solo albums of his own. In 1999 he became the newest member of the Yellowjackets. Peter also has three instructional videos, a performance video titled "Peter Erskine Trio/Live at Jazz Baltica" (Hal Leonard Corporation) as well as two drum instruction books, the most recent entitled "The Drum Perspective," also published by Hal Leonard Corporation.

I have been honored to play with these two wonderful musicians in various settings over the years and they never cease to amaze me with their musicianship and warmth as human beings. I thank them both for their contribution to this project.